Ecosystem Hacking

RYAN LILLY

ECOSYSTEM HACKER MANIFESTO

I help entrepreneurs;
The life-blood of our economy.
I do this work not for my ego,
But for prosperity for people
in a place I'm passionate about.
I believe anyone can be an entrepreneur;
Creativity and courage are color-blind
And combined will conquer any challenge.
My calling is to be a connector;
My greatest contribution the one-to-one and
one-to-many connections I help make.
I am an ecosystem builder;
Seeking-out, synergizing, & supporting
entrepreneurs
While streamlining the startup process
and sharing our collective story.
I am an entrepreneur.
Because I also create within the ecosystem I
build.
And together we're going to make this
ecosystem uniquely awesome.
Let's START!

CONTENTS

ACKNOWLEDGMENTS

To all of the passionate entrepreneurs who have crossed-paths with me on their journey.

To all of the compassionate entrepreneurial ecosystem builders I've met from communities around the world.

To Pamela, Harmony, and Gracie. I love you.

1 WHAT'S NOT WORKING

I believe the greatest opportunity a community can pursue is to serve entrepreneurs pursuing opportunities.

A decade ago I started helping entrepreneurs. Nothing could have prepared me for the characters I would meet and the ideas I would encounter.

From the traditional mom-and-pop small businesses, to the high tech startups, to the most out-there inventions you've ever heard of -- I once famously met with a guy who was convinced he had invented a time machine --

the diversity of ideas has made this journey an interesting one.

When I first started helping entrepreneurs, I have to admit that I suffered from "imposter syndrome." While I had launched a couple of successful online businesses myself, I somehow felt unqualified to be giving people advice.

Not to mention, I was also about 20-30 years younger than some of the entrepreneurs I was meeting with. When one of them would first sit-down to meet with me, I would often get the look of, "Oh great, this kid is supposed to know how I can launch my business idea or scale my company?"

But I sought to prove myself to every entrepreneur I worked with by providing them with something unique -- whether it was some insightful bit of information, or more importantly a connection to someone who was uniquely equipped to help them.

Those connections, I soon realized, were in fact the most powerful gift I could give an entrepreneur. Over time, I built a network of mentors, investors, and others who were the ones really making the difference in these entrepreneurs' lives.

It wasn't always easy. Despite doing my best to help these innovators, they didn't always take my advice. Some didn't want guidance, they wanted resources for something they insisted was flawless.

Others came thinking I would do their work for them or that I had a stack of money behind my desk.

But the ones who went-on to become successful have made it all worth it.

That's what I enjoy most about helping entrepreneurs -- getting to see ideas turned-into reality and lives transformed every day.

There's something so satisfying about how a creative thought can turn-into a tangible product or a viable business. And as someone who helps entrepreneurs for a living, I get to see this creative process happening anew all the time.

I've also discovered I'm not alone. As an ecosystem builder, I've come-across so many inspiring people doing the same around the world.

All of them have had in common that, like me, they love being around creativity and they have a servant's heart which wants nothing more than to help others succeed.

They also understand the impact that entrepreneurs have on the economy – and have "seen the light" that this type of work is the most effective form of economic development in-practice today.

Old School Economic Development

Economies are moving and changing faster than ever, yet most economic development practice has remained the same.

Old-school economic development is primarily about trying to attract large employers (like factories or corporate offices, for example) into your community.

Usually this is done with the help of

financial incentives which your town offers to the company in exchange for them locating there.

But attracting large companies is getting more competitive all the time. Few communities can do it, and those who do encounter this controversial matter of incentives.

Business retention is also part of traditional economic development. The idea here being that a community should focus on keeping the large employers they have, and assist them to do big expansion projects which will add more capacity for jobs.

Still, expansion projects are difficult, they often don't serve to diversify your economy (you're getting more of what you already have), and it may still involve incentives.

...Incentives that require you to justify whether the expansion project would have really happened without your help at all.

Helping entrepreneurs has been an economic development strategy for a long time too, but it has usually been prioritized last after attraction and retention.

In fact, there are many economic developers today who simply pay nice lip service to entrepreneurs. They refer those smaller projects to their local Small Business Development Center or someone else who will have to care for them.

Why has economic development cast entrepreneurs aside in the past? Because economic developers are currently evaluated on one metric more than any other: JOBS.

And because, unfortunately, there's a lot of politics in economic development. So, for an economic developer, the object of the game becomes: "How can I impact the perceived creation of the greatest number of jobs during the current election cycle of the politicians I'm held accountable to?"

But a lot has changed about how this game is played. First, large job projects are becoming harder to come-by because of trends like offshoring and automation.

Projecting long-term out into the future, I believe automation will eventually kill any job which doesn't rely on a human touch or creative thought.

That's why building within the new creative and entrepreneur economy is so important. Because you can't automate creativity or the ability to take risks.

Second, as I read in a recent publication from the Kauffman Foundation, "people are the new companies." In other words, individual entrepreneurs are now able to build entire companies (and wealth for themselves) without hiring a single full-time employee... or at least far fewer employees than they hired before.

Even the largest companies are growing without hiring as many people as in the past.

"In 1962, Kodak employed 75,000 people. In 2013, when Facebook hit the same revenue scale, it employed only 6,300 people."

— Kauffman E-Ship Playbook

Communities are also largely either unaware of this new economy, or they're living in denial of it. Few tackle it consciously.

The bad news is that old school economic development just isn't working anymore.

But the good news is that an amazing new field has emerged to replace traditional economic development called Ecosystem Building.

Too many communities look outward in search of solutions to the economic challenges they face. Too few look inward at the faces of entrepreneurship and innovation right in front of them who have been the solution all-along. That's what Ecosystem Building is about.

<u>Ecosystem Building Defined:</u>

A deliberate process by which a community organizes an effort to serve and grow the entrepreneurs and startups which already exist to some degree inside it.

The Law of New Economy Mastery

When the collective effort that a community puts into ecosystem building becomes greater than effort they once put only into seeking-out and serving large employers (traditional economic development), they will have mastered the new economy.

Ecosystem building is still an emerging field, and because of that it has several challenges. One of the biggest, I believe, is that while there are lots of consultants and models out there which aim to make ecosystem building easier, they aren't currently easy to implement and scale at a fast rate.

In fact, some have said that building an entrepreneurial ecosystem can take 10 years or more. To some degree, I believe that's true. At the core of an ecosystem are trust and collaboration among the people in the ecosystem (entrepreneurs, investors, mentors, service providers, etc.).

Make no mistake that there are no shortcuts to trust and collaboration – they can't be "hacked."

Still, ecosystem builders are expected to deliver results quickly. Many plant seeds that only sprout after years of watering.

However, I have discovered from my experience having done this work for nearly a decade now that ecosystem building is actually a simple process.

It's one which can be broken-down into five easy parts – and within each of those exist systems you can implement and ideas you can experiment with to make ecosystem building happen faster.

And I call this, "Ecosystem Hacking."

<u>Ecosystem Hacking Defined:</u>

Incorporating existing tools and systems to grow your entrepreneurial ecosystem and your economy <u>faster</u>.

At its core, Ecosystem Hacking is about innovation and entrepreneurial thinking within the field of Ecosystem Building.

It also means adapting pieces of solutions and systems from other ecosystems and weaving them together into a solution and a system that serves your unique community and leverages your local entrepreneurial talent the most.

My hope is that in the brief chapters which follow, that you might pickup some idea or nugget of information which speeds the development of you own ecosystem efforts.

At the end of the day, what we're really after is a win-win. A win for the entrepreneurs you serve and the interconnected ecosystem they live in.

2 THINK LIKE AN ENTREPRENEUR TO HELP ENTREPRENEURS

A while ago I was asked to come to another city and figure-out why a business incubator there was failing. It was the first time I had ever been asked for input on someone else's ecosystem building effort, so I felt honored in a way.

I also felt awkward about it and concerned. Entrepreneurial ecosystems are complex. I somehow doubted that I could determine the cause of this incubator's problems in just the few hours I would be there for lunch and a tour.

I was also going covertly. The person who invited me to visit was not the incubator manager, but instead a community leader who felt worried about how this entrepreneur development effort was doing in their city.

This person asked that I come have a look at the program, but not tell the people there that I was doing any kind of evaluation. I was just a "guest" visiting from another city, who wanted to learn what this entrepreneurship stuff was all about.

The incubator was in an old building which had formerly been a school. We walked-into the lobby and at first didn't see anyone. I browsed-around a brochure rack and a few business cards left on the counter of an old receptionist desk.

There was some outdated information about old workshops, brochures on a grant program created back in the 1990's (this was 2017), and business cards strewn-about for the local small business development people and retired mentors.

After five minutes, an older lady came-out from somewhere in the back to greet us. She seemed kind of surprised that someone had actually come-in, like it didn't happen all that often. "I wanted to learn more about your incubator and what you do here," I said.

"Oh, well our incubator manager is in a meeting in the moment, but you're free to look-around," she said.

I began walking-down the labyrinth of old, stale-smelling hallways. I kept passing room-after-empty room. Finally, I came-upon one office with an insurance company's name on the placard outside the door.

I knocked, and asked if they were either new to insurance, or there as a service provider to the other businesses in the building.

"Nope," the middle-aged woman sitting in the office said. "We're just a regular-old insurance company. Been in existence in this town 30 years. Just needed another office to work out of and they had empty space here."

I turned the corner and began walking-down another long corridor of empty offices. I happened-upon one which said "Incubator Manager" outside the door.

The door was open, but the room was dark. I peeked-in and could clearly see a guy sitting in a chair, folded-over, asleep on his desk with drool coming out of his mouth. I'm not making this stuff up. Drool coming out of his mouth!

I made my way back to the lobby and found the receptionist there waiting for me. "Well, what did you think?" she said. "Well, maybe I came on an off-day? I didn't see many businesses. How many do you have in your incubator program?" I said. "She looked anxious for a second, looked-down at her fingers as if to count, and then with a depressed look on her face said, "Well, two. We have two."

I thanked her, walked-out of the building and across the street where I had lunch with the community leader who had invited me there on the spy mission. He had asked three other community leaders to join us for lunch, so that I could give them an outsider's perspective of what I thought might be wrong with their approach to economic development and entrepreneurship.

"How long has that incubator manager been in his position?" I asked.

"Oh, him? Well, he worked in the city's community redevelopment department for years. He was near retirement and looking for something else to do, so we gave him this," one of them, a city councilman, told me.

"Hmm," I replied. "Has he ever started a business himself? Is he an entrepreneur now as well?"

"Nope," one of them said abruptly. "He's been in government most of his life."

"So, what you're telling me," I began slowly, "is that you have someone trying to lead your entrepreneur ecosystem building effort who has no experience as an entrepreneur... and clearly also lacks any kind of passion for it?"

They all stared at me blankly for a second, then I could see the lightbulbs start to click-on in their heads.

I believe that one of the most basic, fundamental truths of entrepreneurial ecosystem building is that the people doing it need to be entrepreneurs themselves, with entrepreneurial mindsets, and a genuine passion for seeing other entrepreneurs succeed.

And by "passion," I mean not only an inward sense of motivation and purpose, but an outwardly contagious energy that inspires others to action.

Being an ecosystem builder isn't like any other "job." It's the opposite of a job. It's an entrepreneurial mindset in itself to innovate within your community by bringing other entrepreneurs together and passionately telling their stories.

If you're reading this book, I expect that's you.

But if you're not reading this book, and your

using it to protect your desk from drool… nevermind.

Think Like an Entrepreneur to Help Them

To transform economies we must transform communities.

To transform communities, we must transform people.

To transform people, we must transform ourselves and our mindsets.

Effectively helping entrepreneurs requires thinking like an entrepreneur. Many would even argue it also requires actually being an entrepreneur.

Would you get on a plane flown by someone who has never piloted one before? If you were an entrepreneur starting-out, would you want the help of someone who had started a business themselves? Of course!

Unfortunately, that's not always the case in entrepreneurial ecosystems. There are many places where the "blind are leading the blind."

There are people in government and economic development, like the one in our opening story, who have never come close to starting a company.

If you've never been an entrepreneur yourself, and have no interest in ever becoming one… and no offense when I say this… but I would suggest reconsidering becoming an ecosystem builder.

You owe it not only to yourself (find something else you're both knowledgeable and passionate about) but you also owe it to the entrepreneurs who need help from someone who has walked the path before.

Know Your Why & Passion

Before starting anything in life or business, be sure you are clear on your "why." What is your true and clear motivation for helping entrepreneurs?

You need this sense of purpose to get you out of bed every morning, and more importantly to generate the passion needed to really make a difference in the lives of

entrepreneurs.

That's because helping entrepreneurs isn't all about "technical assistance." I do "technical assistance" by the way, but I hate that term. Helping entrepreneurs is largely psychological.

Entrepreneurs need positive energy, motivation, and constant building-up. There are ecosystem builders out there who walk around every day in a bad mood. Some are in a constant state of numb bureaucratic malaise. They aren't ecosystem builders, they're ecosystem destroyers.

You've got to bring your whole self to this!

Entrepreneurs are different from employees in that they have learned to bring their authentic selves to what they do. So, if you are less than anything but authentic yourself, you're not going to create any rapport with entrepreneurs whatsoever.

If you're helping entrepreneurs for any other reason than this is your true passion and you actually care about making your community's economy more vibrant and successful, don't do it.

If you need help remembering your "why" for ecosystem building every day, I suggest writing it down and keeping it in front of you at your desk.

Take a look at the manifesto at the beginning of this book and see if it resonates with you and could serve as a reminder.

Never become so busy working at building an ecosystem that you forget why you're helping entrepreneurs in the first place.

And if you can't remember why, or you can't state it clearly, stop everything you're doing until you've reconnected with that.

Vision

The worst thing that can happen to an economy of any size is for the majority of people in it to lose hope in its ability to make a comeback.

Sometimes an Ecosystem Hacker must first do the emotional and leadership work involved in restoring hope. That's where a vision comes in from the beginning.

What do you want your local entrepreneurial ecosystem to look like a year from now? Ten years from now? How will you get there?

Stephen Covey said, "Begin with the end in-mind." So, starting at the 10-year vision and working backwards, what specific actions would you need to take now to get there?

Few communities have a specific definition of economic development. If they have a definition, fewer have built community consensus and vision around it. In the rare case a community has both a definition and consensus, fewer still have a bold-enough strategy and courageous-enough leadership needed to honor that definition of economic development as a verb to be taken action upon.

Bootstrap

Would-be entrepreneurs often cite a lack of resources (capital, talent, etc.) as the reason they don't take action and start their business. Would-be ecosystem builders often focus on a lack of community resources with similar names (investment, workforce, etc.).

Successful entrepreneurs and ecosystem builders are ones who realize they must start where they are, with what they have, right NOW.

You don't need a grant, a giant facility, or fancy branding to help entrepreneurs. You need to start helping them with what you have.

Helping entrepreneurs make connections within the ecosystem, the primary role of an ecosystem builder, doesn't have to take any money at all.

In fact, you can start doing it right now, where you are. Try this exercise: Think of an entrepreneur in your ecosystem who you feel has great potential but is struggling to get started or grow (this should be easy).

Ask that entrepreneur who it would be helpful for them to meet. Mentors? Investors? How about customers!? Now think of a few people you know who may fit these descriptions. Really brainstorm around your current network and who may be a good fit.

Once you have contacts in-mind, open a new email or message in LinkedIn, and make an introduction of the entrepreneur to a few of those people.

Chances are, not every one of those connections will bear fruit. In fact, maybe only one of them will turn into something really valuable for the entrepreneur. But the point I'm making here is this: That exercise didn't cost you anything but a few minutes and a couple of clicks.

There is such a huge myth out there that this work takes lots of time and money. It doesn't. As we saw in this exercise, it just takes creatively using your existing relationships to intentionally make connections for the entrepreneurs who need them.

As you get better at doing this, and scale your ecosystem building efforts, you *will* likely run-into needs for capital. But if you're truly being successful at ecosystem building and adding value to entrepreneurs, then finding those resources should come much more easily.

The ecosystem builders who always seem to be in a struggle for funding are likely the ones who are either not already adding value in their ecosystem or not clearly communicating that value to others.

I always advise startups not to take on any debt or equity investors at the very beginning, if they can help it. Debt and equity both make you responsible to satisfying someone other than your customers, who should be your main focus as you determine if your business model will even work. Then, use capital to scale later on.

Likewise, if you start ecosystem building with a loan on a big facility, a grant from a government agency, etc. your focus will become paying back that loan or meeting those grant reporting requirements -- both of which require time and energy you need to devote at the beginning to your customer (the entrepreneur).

In fact, I've met people helping entrepreneurs who seem so focused on grant writing and/or reporting that the time they spend actually helping entrepreneurs (doing the actual work) is miniscule. If an entrepreneur did that, they would be out of business!

Outside capital can be a great resource to scale an already successful ecosystem building effort, but my advice is to avoid it at the very start if possible.

If it's too late for that and you're already operating under a grant or ongoing financial support from another agency, find someone to delegate that reporting to so that you can focus on what matters -- finding ways of making connections for entrepreneurs.

Ecosystem Hacker Time Management:

You need to spend 80% of your time on helping entrepreneurs make connections, and 20% or less of your time on administrative crap like grant reporting.

Bootstrapping is ultimately about

resourcefulness and being creative with what you have. Great ecosystem builders do this all the time. They take an old building, for example, and turn it into a gathering place for entrepreneurs without doing a lot of expensive work to it.

A great analogy for this is one of an artificial coral reef. In an effort to save a struggling tropical ecosystem, marine biologists will sink things like old farm equipment, boats, and even school buses to the bottom of the ocean floor. Coral will begin attaching-themselves to the structures, and before long you have a colorful, vibrant new ecosystem.

Many startup ecosystems get started in artificial reefs -- they grow on and out-of the physical remains of the last economy.

That's a great lead-in to our next key to an Ecosystem Hacker Mindset…

Innovation

The biggest constraint on a community's economy is NOT quality of life, available workforce, or even the alignment of its political and organizational leadership. It's the collective mindset of its entrepreneurs and their appetite for the inevitable risk that comes with radical innovation.

Most old-school economic developers are trying the same things over and over, expecting to get a different result.

Tech startups teach us to constantly measure our results, learn from them, and if needed try something else.

Innovate! Like an entrepreneur, as an ecosystem builder, you must give yourself permission to try things and fail.

Because there's no cookie-cutter approach to ecosystem building, you must try different methods and programs for helping entrepreneurs.

Some of these might be things you've seen done successfully in other communities, while others might be creations of your own.

Either way, there's a great chance they might fail when you try to apply them in your community. That failure is just part of this work -- like building a company.

For entrepreneurs, failure is only a problem because it affects their own success (it affects them the most). For us as ecosystem builders, failure is an even bigger problem because we have this whole network of stakeholders.

In other words, we're striving to be entrepreneurial / innovative within a traditional / bureaucratic hierarchy.

If you work for a politician, government agency, or an old-school non-profit, ask yourself if you REALLY feel permission to fail.

If you don't, address that with yourself and those you're reporting to. Make sure you're both clear on the fact that helping entrepreneurs requires thinking and acting like an entrepreneur -- and that means taking on risk, trying new things, and failing until you get it right.

In times of economic uncertainty, many

communities find ways to seek certainty. Successful communities find ways to play in the sandbox of uncertainty that already exists.

A community's cry for certainty and control over its circumstances is often what inhibits ideas and innovation the most. We need to get our communities comfortable with being uncomfortable -- because more change is coming.

Darwinian Economic Development:

It is not the strongest or largest cities that will survive the new economy, but those that are most adaptive to change.

Ecosystem builders who have not adopted an entrepreneur mindset (or who are not entrepreneurs themselves) constantly try to avoid and minimize risk.

Let's be honest here: in those cases they often end-up fudging the numbers and writing fluffy narratives in their reporting to cover-up or justify what a true entrepreneur would have been brave-enough to call failure.

I'll give you an example. I know someone who managed an incubation program, operating under a state grant. They launched a shiny new program to help entrepreneurs, which didn't turn-out to be all that successful (they were guessing what entrepreneurs in their ecosystem needed, rather than really listening to them -- we'll talk about that later).

When it came to reporting on the success of that program in the quarterly grant reports, the ecosystem builder would fluff-up their failure and fudge their numbers, making them appear very successful.

If they did otherwise, and admitted failure on the current program, they felt they would lose funding.

As a community of ecosystem builders, we have to get ourselves out of this risk-avoidance and self-justification mindset. It's not sustainable and it's not helping anyone.

If you're doing either of these, you're not doing justice to the people you should be helping, and you're ultimately just lying to yourself. Not to mention the fact that doing this will only get you so far -- before long the success or failure of an ecosystem will speak for itself and no amount of number fudging will convince people otherwise.

When it comes to innovation remember: The greatest enemy of any type of economic development isn't outsourcing, automation, or the rise of ecommerce. It's complacency and a failure to innovate. And the economic impact of any type of economic development (ecosystem building or otherwise) is always directly proportional to the innovations you implement.

At the end of the day, a community reinvents itself by inventing new ways to serve the entrepreneurs who call the community home. And that's what Ecosystem Hacking is about.

Lean (Build-Measure-Learn)

The same "Lean Startup" model that many ecosystem builders encourage their entrepreneurs to use is the one we should be using ourselves.

Lean Startup teaches entrepreneurs to come-up with a Minimally Viable Product (MVP), to test it on customers, measure those results, and iterate the design again.

Many ecosystem builders are going about helping entrepreneurs in the exact opposite way. They're creating programs marketed as being "perfect" from the very beginning, deploying them to their entire community of entrepreneurs without any beta testing whatsoever, and are not incorporating feedback into the design of these programs.

So why aren't ecosystem builders adopting lean startup principles in their own work? I think it has a lot to do with what we just talked about in the previous section.

We must give ourselves permission to fail! If you're beholden to any kind of political stakeholder (for example, a city council or county commission), realize that ecosystem building means trying new things and that those things will occasionally not work out.

Ecosystem Builders must be brave-enough to try new things, smart-enough to tell if those things are working, and humble-enough to call a failed experiment for what it is… before trying again.

Build a Team

An entrepreneurial community isn't built by one person working in isolation over the span of a weekend. It's built by a tribe working towards a common goal they care passionately about over the span years.

Just like startups must build a team, you too must build a team in order to build a startup ecosystem.

At the end of the day, there is only so much you can do alone. In order to have a real impact, and for your effort to scale, you're going to need to enlist the help of others in your ecosystem building mission.

Find other people who are already helping entrepreneurs. They may not yet call themselves ecosystem builders - or have any idea what that term even means yet - but they have a common interest in helping entrepreneurs be successful.

Try to find people doing this who don't necessarily have a financial interest in doing so. In other words, you may want to avoid consultants who are only interested in finding clients.

Find other entrepreneurs who also seem to take an active role in leading or facilitating events. Invite them to lunch and tell them you want to partner with them in a more intentional effort to build your entrepreneurial ecosystem.

Be sure to build an ecosystem building team which is diverse, so that you can build a diverse ecosystem.

In other words, recruit builders of all races, genders, ages, orientations, etc. The more diverse your team, the more impact you'll be able to have on the ecosystem, and the healthier it will be as a result.

Meet regularly with one-another and create a local Facebook group or Slack channel dedicated to entrepreneurial ecosystem building in your community.

Persuasiveness

The difference between an inventor and an entrepreneur is the willingness and ability to sell what they've created.

Likewise, the difference between someone who designs great entrepreneur programs and someone who successfully implements and grows them is the ability to sell those programs to others -- and to do that they have to have actual VALUE for entrepreneurs.

If you're offering workshops for entrepreneurs and none are coming, it may not be a marketing problem -- it may be a value problem. Be a "Purple Cow" in the words of author Seth Godin and become something that everyone in your community is talking about.

Build Systems

One of the best entrepreneurship books I've ever read was The E-Myth by Michael Gerber.

In it, Gerber talks about going from

working "in" your business to "on" your business.

His message really is this: how can you step-away from being the technician in your business - the person who makes the product or service - to become the person who implements systems and thinks like a franchise owner to scale your business faster?

As Ecosystem Hackers wanting to go faster, we must keep this same principle of system building in-mind. An ecosystem is, afterall, a system! In fact, it's a system made-up of sub-systems.

So, if we want our ecosystem to really scale, we need to create efficient systems underneath it which make things happen more automatically and independent of our direct efforts.

What are the most frequent tasks you undertake to help entrepreneurs? When it comes to connecting them or sharing their stories, as an example, what about that task takes most of your time?

Is it sending an email introduction of one entrepreneur to another? Is there something you do before or after your meeting with an entrepreneur that always takes a long time?

Get creative, think like an entrepreneur, and either find a system or create a system which can make that thing happen faster.

Many daily functions and common requests made of an ecosystem team can now be systematized to automatically happen on their own, allowing you to do what matters most... facilitating connections, innovating, and telling a great story.

One of an Ecosystem Hacker's primary jobs is to put themselves out of the jobs they take-on. If something is truly valuable to entrepreneurs in your community, it can only be sustained long-term if the entrepreneurs take ownership of it and make it their own.

And that happens easiest when you design a system which allows them to take it over and run it the same as you did.

Leverage systems for your ecosystem

hacking team to communicate (Slack), manage projects (Trello), and tell stories (YouTube, Facebook Live, Medium, etc.)

Your ecosystem doesn't have problems, it has opportunities for innovation and systemization.

Execute!

Today, most communities are their own worst enemies. They fail to advance their local economy for the same reason they fail to advance everything else: They spend too much time talking and not enough time executing.

Don't plan to help entrepreneurs. Go out and actually do it. Even if you don't know exactly what to start with, just do something and see where it takes you.

Action creates momentum, and momentum is something so many ecosystem building efforts could use at the start!

Most communities take a reactionary approach to economic development, attempting to fix what they perceive is currently broken. The best communities anticipate future economic trends and become proactive in preparing for them in advance. Wayne Gretzky once said, "Skate to where the puck is going, not to where it is."

Get out ahead of where this new economy is going and start helping entrepreneurs today!

In the next 5 chapter's we'll look at the Ecosystem Hacker Model for doing this:

Seek, Synergize, Support, Streamline, Share

5 Action Checklist

☐ Know and **write-down your "why"** for helping entrepreneurs. Keep it at your desk.

☐ Bootstrap. Stop looking for money and start looking for entrepreneurs to connect. **Write down one entrepreneur's name.** Ask them to tell you 3 people (or types of people) they would like to meet to grow their business. Then go-out and find them. Facilitate the introduction. Repeat.

☐ Build a Team. **Make a list of 10 people in your community you think could help your effort.** Call or email them and set a meeting date for lunch. Setup a Facebook page or Slack Channel to communicate on together.

☐ Innovate. Brainstorm a list of 10 **ideas for your ecosystem.** What things are not functioning well in your ecosystem right now? What idea(s) might solve that problem. Think like an entrepreneur to help entrepreneurs.

☐　Create & Utilize Systems. **Setup a list of tasks for the team in a Google Doc, Trello board, etc.** Make sure you think in terms of "systems" for the remaining chapters in this book.

3 SEEK

About seven years ago I was helping entrepreneurs in the rural Midwest. And when I say rural, I mean there were cornfields in every direction. One of my biggest concerns initially was, "Where in the heck are we going to find entrepreneurs out here?"

One of my colleagues at the time believed that the best way to really get to know an area was to drive around. Rather than sit behind a desk and try to figure things out, he was all about getting in the car and exploring.

One day we drove about 15 minutes to a small, neighboring town. As we crossed-over into the outskirts of town, we passed a Hardee's restaurant. It seemed like a promising sign of civilization. But as we continued into downtown, things started to get weird.

Really weird.

The moment we drove-onto Main Street, we could both feel this eerie silence. One hundred-year-old shops, most of them two and three stories high, lined both sides of the street -- every single one of them empty.

There were no cars on the street other than the one we were in. The only other thing on wheels was a riding lawnmower someone had parked in the middle of the road. It looked almost as out-of-place as we did.

We parked, got-out of the car, and just stared at one-another for about thirty seconds in the dead silence.

I fully expected at any moment Rod Sterling would step-out into the street with a cigarette clenched between his teeth and tell us we had just crossed-over into the Twilight Zone.

We walked to one end of the road to find the only sign of activity: a bar with neon lights flashing and a church that appeared to still have some activity. The bar and church seemed symbolic of the two ways people cope with disruption in their lives.

Right next to those two buildings, in the middle of the street at one end, was an old World War II-era cannon with a badly-faded plaque on it.

My colleague remarked that it was the proverbial cannon we could fire down the middle of the street... and no one would care. Because no one was there.

I pulled-out my phone, surprised to see I actually had a wireless signal of one tiny, measly bar. I went to Wikipedia, determined to figure-out what had happened in this ghost town.

It took a minute to load, but finally an all-to-familiar story appeared. This once-bustling town had been home to a leading glass manufacturer. Then, one day, it all stopped.

And the town stopped with it.

Feeling more than a little depressed, we began walking back to our car to drive back to the office.

Just then an old man appeared, stumbling out of the bar, and walking towards the riding lawnmower in the middle of the street-- it appeared he was going home too.

As he crossed the street ahead of us, he looked-over somewhat confused. His gaze was also one of helplessness. He seemed to be saying with his eyes, "I'm one of the lone survivors on this ghost town, and I've given up hope."

Back in the car, my coworker and I discussed the dismal prospects of finding any sort of innovation or entrepreneurship in this place to work with.

Most frightening to think about was the fact that we had several other towns around us just like this one -- places which were, for all-intents-and-purposes, almost completely dead economically.

We started to drive back to the office, and then decided to go-down a little side street to have a look at a residential area.

Most of the homes were boarded-up and falling apart. A few seemed to have activity, but questionable activity at that.

As we were driving, we suddenly spotted something odd-looking up in the distance.

"Hey, slow down a bit. What's that?" I said.

It looked like some kind of bicycle being ridden in the road up-ahead... but this bike had been highly modified and had all kinds of stuff attached to it.

As we pulled-up slowly behind the weird-looking-contraption, the bicyclist pulled-over to the side, stopped, and just looked at us. I rolled-down my passenger-side window, anxious to figure-out what the heck this thing was.

The bicycle and its rider both appeared to be about fifty years-old. A black vinyl enclosure -- a canopy of sorts -- surrounded the bike on three sides.

On top of the canopy's roof was a very small solar panel, about the size of a notebook. Underneath the canopy, above the bicyclist's head, was an LED light and a small fan to blow air.

"Hey, we like your bike," I said, not quite sure at first of exactly what I was seeing.

"Oh, thanks. I made all of this myself! The solar panel powers the light and the fan. I can ride in the dark and stay cool in the summer. I've been tinkering with this thing for years."

At that moment I noticed something else on the roof of his canopy, which I had missed before. It was a large, black, rubber rat with red eyes. Like the kind you would find at a novelty or gag gift store.

"Uh, is that a toy rat on top of your canopy?" I said.

"Yeah, his name is Herbert," the bicyclist responded proudly.

"Does he do something? Is he part of the design somehow?" I asked.

"Nope, he doesn't do anything. He just squeaks. Want to hear?"

"Uh, no, that's OK..." I started.

Before I could finish my sentence the cyclist kicked-down his kickstand, and abruptly stood-up.

He reached on top of the canopy to where Herbert the rat was fastened to the roof with a wire tie. The rubber rat let-out a loud squealing noise as he squeezed it — a squeak that echoed through the neighborhood, like a squeaky dog toy into a megaphone.

I don't know how, but I kept a straight face.

"Hey, here's my business card," I said. "Thanks for showing us your bike. We'll be in touch?"

We rolled-up our windows and laughed harder than we had ever laughed in our lives on the way back to the office. Literally, I laughed so hard that I was crying and gasping for breath.

We had found innovation where we least expected it. We had found someone working with solar technology in the middle of a near ghost town!

And we had also found Herbert. The squeaky rat who didn't serve a purpose other than to bring his inventor friend joy on the journey.

I realized that day for the first time that innovation is absolutely everywhere.

EVERYWHERE!

Even where you least expect it.

The first step in growing an economy with entrepreneurs is to go out and find them.

While some entrepreneurs in your community might be higher-profile than others, there are always so many more behind the scenes going unnoticed.

Seeking-out entrepreneurs means evaluating what you can plainly see in the ecosystem and eliciting entrepreneurs to come to you.

Evaluate (What you can see.)

Look around you. Who are the entrepreneurs in every industry of your community who seem to be shaking things up? Who are the disruptors?

Begin making a list or tracking them in a shared Google Doc. Be sure that others on your ecosystem-building team are contributing to this list as well.

As you find these entrepreneurs, also ask who <u>they know</u> who you should talk to in the entrepreneur community.

Who are their friends, and what meetings do they attend together? Are there certain Meetups they enjoy? If so, go check them out! Start pulling these threads and soon the existing ecosystem will begin to unravel.

I'm a big fan of Seth Godin's book The

Purple Cow. The big takeaway for me after reading it was:

Rather than focus on traditional advertising, a company should first seek to be truly innovative. If it is innovative, it will be remarkable. If it's remarkable, word of it will spread quickly... and word-of-mouth is the best form of marketing you can have going for your company.

As you think about finding entrepreneurs, I first suggest making sure your ecosystem effort is a Purple Cow.

In other words, is the result you create for entrepreneurs — your value proposition — really novel/unique/differentiated?

If you ran a business incubator and an entrepreneur saw your incubator next to ten other startup development programs in the ecosystem, why would yours stick out to them? Why would they want to immediately reach out to you?

The innovativeness of an entrepreneur development program will lead directly to success stories from those you help.

And those success stories, if truly powerful enough, should lead to new entrepreneurs seeking you out.

Success, if it's strong enough for long enough, speaks for itself.

But in my experience, when an ecosystem builder is completely new and doesn't have many stories to tell yet, entrepreneurs won't automatically flock to you. You still have to go find them.

Beyond posting flyers, writing press releases, and crafting catchy social media posts, how can you actually "shake the entrepreneurs out of the bushes" and get them to see what your team can do to help them?

10 Ways I've Found Entrepreneurs

1. Put a Call Out on Social Media

This almost sounds too simplistic, but sometimes you have not because you ask not. Start asking people to introduce you to

entrepreneurs.

Post something to social media along the lines of, "I'm looking for entrepreneurs (people starting businesses) in [insert your location name here] as part of an effort to connect and serve them. Would you have any connections for me?"

2. Patent Search

Step 1: Go to the USPTO website: http://patft.uspto.gov/netahtml/PTO/search-adv.htm

Step 2: In the Query box, type: IC/City (Replace "City" with your town's name).

Step 3: Starting from the top of the list (patents issued most recently) look for patents from local inventors.

Note their name, track-down their contact information (LinkedIn or Facebook), and then reach-out to see if you can help.

3. LinkedIn Search

Step 1: Go to LinkedIn.

Step 2: In the search box at the top-left type "Entrepreneur" or "Inventor". Then, on the right-hand side, click Locations, Click Add, and type your town's name.

Step 3: Look-through the list of people, connect, and introduce yourself!

4. Crowdfunding Sites & Angel List

Step 1: On a crowdfunding site like Kickstarter or IndieGoGo – or on an angel investment website like Gust or Angel.Co (where you must also be logged-in for this to work), type your town's name into the main search box.

Step 2: Click on the individual projects which result and find-out who the creator is for each one.

Step 3: Establish contact via the website's message tool or by looking their name up on a social media site.

5. Business License Registrations

Step 1: If your city or county requires a business or occupational license, find-out where records of recent applications are normally posted (typically in a local newspaper and/or on their website.)

You might also find a way to search incorporation filings at the state-level, and narrow the search to recent filings in your town/city.

Step 2: Scan these lists periodically for new businesses which sound like they may want to connect with you.

Step 3: Establish contact with the entrepreneurs you are interested in via social media. (Hopefully you're noticing a pattern here…)

6. Google & Twitter Alerts

Step 1: Setup both a Google Alert (https://www.google.com/alerts) and a Twitter Alert (https://www.twilert.com/) for search terms including: "Your City's Name" + ["Entrepreneur" and/or +

"Startup" and/or + "Inventor"].

This way, whenever your city's name is mentioned in conjunction with one of these keywords anywhere online, you'll get an email about it.

Step 2: Opt-in to receive a digest of alerts either daily or weekly.

Step 3: If you come-across a tweet or new content via Google which seems like it may be from an area entrepreneur… you guessed it… reach-out using social media. It's the fastest and most likely way to get a response.

7. Meetups & Mixers

Step 1: Go to http://www.meetup.com/ and search for entrepreneur, inventor, and tech meetups in your area. (You may think you know all of them, but just try it!)

Step 2: If you find a meetup you're not familiar with (I did!) RSVP to attend. (P.S. If you don't find a meetup, create one!)

Step 3: Network, network, network. And if you find a Meetup group needing a new place to meet, offer them your place if you have one! (We once discovered a small local tech group was meeting at a restaurant. Now they meet at our incubator facility, and we've gained four new incubator clients as a result.)

8. Craigslist (Yes, Craigslist… this actually works for me.)

Step 1: Go to https://craigslist.org and make sure to select either your town or the area closest to yours.

Step 2: Click "post to classifieds" at the top left to create a new listing (for free). Create your listing under the category: Service Offered > Small Biz Ads

Step 3: Title your ad something like "We help entrepreneurs in [insert city name]." Craigslist will also allow you to attach a photos to your post.

You might choose to include your program's logo, a screenshot of your flyer, and interior shots of your facility. In all forms of marketing, I also recommend including a few testimonials from entrepreneurs you've worked with (given an entrepreneur's permission to do so, of course).

9. Tradeshows

Step 1: Go to a tradeshow database like this one: http://www.expodatabase.com/trade-shows-america/usa/

Step 2: Search either an industry you're interested in connecting with entrepreneurs in (i.e. IT) OR lookup all shows coming to a city in your region.

Step 3: Register for a show as an attendee. DO NOT pay for one of those expensive booths. Walk the floor of the show, and you may just find a few entrepreneurs in the crowd pitching their products for the first time. Bring plenty of business cards and program brochures.

10. Get to really know the touchpoints.

A touchpoint is anyone an entrepreneur may come into contact with in the process of starting their business. A list of these can be found in Chapter 5, but include people like accountants and attorneys.

One of the best referral sources will be investors. One friend who runs an incubator program has told me that he receives more leads from investors than anyone else – because those investors know that his program can vastly improve his portfolio's chance of success.

Invite these touchpoint contacts to lunch and get to know them. If you work together, you can create a win-win for both of you.

The easy part is doing all of these things just once. The hard part is doing all of these consistently.

In fact, I recommend scheduling time on your calendar to conduct the above searches at least once a month to find new entrepreneurs to reach-out to.

If your ecosystem effort makes use of interns or volunteers, having them work on these outreach efforts will be a great lesson in marketing for them (not to mention a time saver for you.)

But in the end remember: Do an outstanding job of meeting and exceeding the needs of the entrepreneurs you find… and you'll one day become a Purple Cow who won't need to find anyone at all. They'll find you.

Tools for Benchmarking & Mapping

Startup Genome Project -- measures "the lifecycle of an ecosystem to deliver a roadmap for any city to take action." More on benchmarking at: https://startupgenome.com/

SourceLink Mapping – works "with a community to quickly understand and assess regional assets available to the entrepreneur." More at: https://www.joinsourcelink.com/

Global Entrepreneurship Network's Ecosystem Connections Mapping Project – "aims to advance both understanding and support for entrepreneurs by creating the largest and best-maintained database of connections among key actors within startup ecosystems around the world." More at: https://genglobal.org/gern/ecosystem-connections-mapping

Elicit (Get them to come to you.)

For every entrepreneur you can see in your community, there are likely ten more you can't see. They're creating companies quietly from their homes, garages, and on their laptops in coffee shops.

So, if you can't see those people, how would you ever hope to connect with them? By drawing them out -- eliciting their attention with something they need.

In other words, what kind of bait works on entrepreneurs? To answer that question, consider first what entrepreneurs really want and need...

First and foremost, entrepreneurs need **connections** -- to customers, partners, potential employees, investors, service providers… you name it.

As an entrepreneurial ecosystem builder, the number one skill you should be developing is the ability to make connections in your community.

Being able to introduce an entrepreneur to someone they need to speak to will serve them better than anything else you could ever do for them. So, to find entrepreneurs, one of your core marketing messages should be that you have the network and connections to help them succeed.

Entrepreneurs also need **knowledge** -- many times in the form of how to do business. Most of the entrepreneurs you meet will already have great knowledge about their product or service.

But they will likely be weaker on knowledge about how to do business -- namely how to market themselves effectively, target customers and make sales.

If you have that knowledge yourself (and as an ecosystem builder, you should) then this is a huge asset you have to offer.

After connections and knowledge, the remaining needs entrepreneurs will most commonly have include more **tangible resources** like capital, equipment, or physical space.

Often, ecosystem builders will make the mistake of leading with these things when trying to elicit entrepreneurs from their community. In reality, the first two items -- connections and knowledge -- are far more powerful.

In fact, today it's possible to start a business with little-to-no capital and no permanent physical space for a company to call their own. Still, these things can generate interest and in many communities they are indeed still needed.

5 Action Checklist

☐ Get up from behind your desk, **get into your car or go for a walk to a place within your community you've never been to**. Start talking to random people you've never spoken to there. Develop "innovation goggles" for yourself – and lookout for innovation around you where you least expect it.

☐ **Search for entrepreneurs in your community online**, using one or more of the methods in this chapter. Create a list of at least 10 you've never heard of before. As an ecosystem building team, start building a list of entrepreneurs or inviting them into a group.

☐ **Benchmark your ecosystem and/or create a basic map** as you discover more of it. Use one of the resources listed in the Benchmarking & Mapping section, or create your own if you're on a budget.

☐ Your super power (and the thing you most need to market) as an ecosystem builder is your ability to make valuable connections.

Find ways to market and leverage your existing network of contacts in order to find entrepreneurs. For example, **email accountants, attorneys, and other business service providers to see if they know of any entrepreneurs.** Ask them to keep an eye-out and send you referrals.

☐ **Create a free information product which every entrepreneur in your community would find valuable**.

Whether it's a white paper on what most determines success for entrepreneurs in your area, or a collection of interviews with inspiring local entrepreneurs, put something on paper you can use as a lead magnet to draw entrepreneurs to your team.

At the end of the document, include a link and information about your ecosystem building efforts and how to connect. The example of a "Hitchhiker's

Guide" found later in Chapter 6 is an example of content meant to both help entrepreneurs and bring them into your community.

4 SYNERGIZE

The weekend of our big hackathon was finally here. I had been planning this event for over two months. After securing a sponsorship, I pumped money into Facebook ads like crazy to draw participants to our incubator facility for a fun-filled weekend of building cool apps together.

I had been a part of Startup Weekends and hackathons in other cities, and I was excited to finally be organizing one of my own. Registration was free, and to entice attendees, I promoted that free food would be served throughout the weekend. The guest list quickly grew to over forty people. I was stoked.

The morning of the hackathon, I waited in our largest conference room at the incubator for all of our guests to arrive.

One or two trickled-in. Then another and another. By the start time, however, there were only about ten people in the room -- only 25% of those who had RSVP'd.

My stomach dropped. How embarrassing. A hackathon promoted to this level, and all we had to show for it is ten people!?

I contemplated telling everyone in the room to pack-up and head-home -- that we would try this again some other time. Then I suddenly remembered a quote from Margaret Mead.

"Never doubt that a small group of thoughtful, committed citizens can change the world; indeed, it's the only thing that ever has."

I also remembered that I had already placed all of the food orders for lunch and dinner throughout the weekend and had pre-paid for most of them.

So, I decided to press-on. I gave a brief set of instructions and house rules to the participants, and then everyone broke-into teams based on the ideas they would work on over the weekend.

When lunch showed-up, we had enough beef brisket to feed forty people. We all laughed at the mountain of food on the conference room table that we somehow had to eat. But the participants were hungry and managed to scarf most of it down.

"Hey Ryan, this is great!" one of them said. "Can you over-order on food like this every time we have an event? I feel like a King!"

As the day went-on, that small group of ten people had a lot of fun together. And they created some pretty cool things that weekend - - from plans for an aquaponics system, to a sensor and software that monitored how many times a door had been opened.

Several of the attendees became good friends during that event too. At least three new companies emerged. Two of them took-up residence in our business incubator.

What started-out feeling like a failure of an event became a testament to the power of innovators colliding with one-another in a collaborative setting.

I realized for the first time that synergy -- whether in one-on-one interactions, large events, or very small gatherings like this one -- is at the very core of ecosystem building.

Well, synergy and about ten pounds of brisket.

Once you've sought-out entrepreneurs, the next step is to "synergize" them together -- intentionally bring them into the same physical or virtual spaces.

The best ecosystem builders don't do anything per se, they serve the people "doing the doing" by connecting them to their real needs and, most importantly, <u>to one another</u>.

The best visualization of this would be two atoms colliding with one another, and the enormous energy that results.

In the world of helping entrepreneurs, collision is a term which refers to intentionally connecting entrepreneurs to one-another and creating spaces in which these chance meetings more occur more spontaneously.

The most fertile ground for an entrepreneur is a connected community committed to cultivating companies by convening collaboration.

There's an old television commercial from the 1970's for Reese's Peanut Butter Cups. Two guys are walking towards one-another on the same side of a sidewalk. One is eating chocolate and the other peanut butter.

Neither is paying any attention to what's in front of them. They run-into one another, one getting chocolate on the other's peanut butter... and the other getting peanut butter on the other's chocolate.

They each take a bite and discover that their new invention tastes delicious, and thus the famous Reese's Peanut Butter Cup is born.

In a healthy entrepreneurial ecosystem, these collisions are *exactly* the sort of interaction we want to see happen.

In the business incubator I run, our companies tend to collaborate with 2-3 other companies in our facility during their incubation period. Often, those collaborative projects result in new products or entirely new companies.

And what's so cool is that those projects and companies are often far more innovative and scalable than what each entrepreneur had been working on by themselves. That is the power of synergy!

So, let's look at how to create intentional collisions…

Entwine (personal intros YOU make)

Personal intros are one of the most common means of communication for an ecosystem builder.

You've just met an entrepreneur who

needs a connection to a potential co-founder and you have someone great in mind. You send an email introducing the two of them and sharing their contact information so they can talk. Or, you might invite them to lunch together. In either case, you're serving the critical role of the convener.

Every person has at least one innovative idea; but not every innovative idea has one person to make it a reality. Sometimes we have to help idea people meet business/execution people. It's like being a personal matchmaker!

The more you make these connections, the easier and more natural it will come. Not every introduction you make will lead to a productive relationship.

In fact, the majority of them may not go anywhere at all. But a few will lead to something special. And they'll make the failures worth it.

Make sure you track these introductions.

One of the most powerful yet underused metrics in ecosystem building is: How many people did you connect, and what new economic value was created in your community as a result of those connections?

Creating Collision Mechanisms

Events

1 Million Cups

One of my biggest regrets as an ecosystem builder is that I did not become involved in 1 Million Cups (1MC) sooner. Created by the Kauffman Foundation, 1MC is now in over 140 cities across the U.S.

Held in most communities every Wednesday morning, it's an opportunity for the entire community to come-out and hear from two local entrepreneurs.

What's so powerful about 1MC though is that it's not necessarily about "pitching" or selling your idea -- it's about getting feedback and creating connections (networking) in your community.

Each week, 1MC accounts for a huge

percentage of the connections that get made in our entrepreneurial community.

Best of all, it's completely free. It was free for us to bring to our community, all of the marketing materials are provided for free, and both attending and presenting are free for entrepreneurs.

The event has also been responsible for helping us spur much-needed diversity in our ecosystem. If you talk to any 1MC organizer they will tell you that this program is very intentional about bringing diverse people together to support entrepreneurs.

You can learn more about 1 Million Cups by visiting www.1MillionCups.com

Startup Weekend

"Startup Weekend is a 54-hour weekend event, during which groups of developers, business managers, startup enthusiasts, marketing gurus, graphic artists and more pitch ideas for new startup companies, form teams around those ideas, and work to develop a working prototype, demo, or presentation by

Sunday evening." *(Source: Wikipedia)* Visit StartupWeekend.com for more details.

Competitions (Pitch Events)

Pitch competitions are a great way to bring entrepreneurs together. Here are a few reasons why:

- There is usually prize money in a pitch competition. Entrepreneurs need money, so it gets them out into the community where before they may have been working in isolation.

- Pitches are a great way to get valuable feedback.

- It's an opportunity for entrepreneurs to clarify and codify their pitch -- communicating it as concisely as possible.

- It's an excellent networking opportunity. You never know who's in the audience.

- Pitches are fun! Entrepreneurs love to

compete. Pitch competitions gamify the startup process.

For the last five years, I've organized an annual youth business pitch competition with about $10,000 in prize money provided by local sponsors.

We didn't start out with that much in prizes initially. But as the competition gained steam and popularity in the area, we had more companies wanting to sponsor and it really took-off.

The first year of the pitch competition I had an experience that I've never forgotten. I had just delivered a short presentation about the contest to a high school class.

After I was done, and the bell had rung, a kid came-up to me and said, "Mr. Lilly, I've had all kinds of business ideas. But my problem is that my parents and teachers have always told me those ideas are stupid, and to concentrate instead on my school work."

It was one of the saddest things I've heard in my life. But it was also one of the happiest feelings I had ever had when I saw him walk-across the stage as a finalist in our pitch competition.

Paid services (systems) have now been created like Reviewr.com that allow you to manage these pitch competitions.

If you're interested in learning more-in-depth about how to put one of these pitch competitions together, checkout my book "How to Start a High School Business Plan Competition" available on Amazon.

Local Entrepreneur Award Ceremonies

There's a saying that you should reward and celebrate that which you want to see more of. If you want more entrepreneurship in your community, find ways of publicly rewarding entrepreneurs for their accomplishments.

Put entrepreneurs on a high pedestal for others in the community to see. The idea is that their friends and neighbors will see them, admire them, and perhaps also think, "Hey, I want to be an entrepreneur too!"

Many communities do some kind of business award ceremony once a year, but not every community gives enough recognition to the startups. I would recommend a startup-only award program, where you focus on a few different categories of startups and different types of entrepreneurs (i.e. Healthcare Startup of the Year, or Young Entrepreneur of the Year).

Aside from bringing entrepreneurs together (synergy – what we're talking about in this chapter), awards shows like these also inspire more would-be entrepreneurs to get started and help tell your community's story as a whole – more on that in Chapter 7.

Food

It may not sound like a big deal, but food is one of those weird things that brings an ecosystem together. Anytime I've ever organized an event for entrepreneurs which provided free food, our attendance has been much higher than the same event when we haven't provided food.

But here's the problem: food can be

expensive - especially if you're feeding lots of hungry entrepreneurs who may be living off of Ramen Noodles.

So, if you don't have a budget or sponsors to help, you should seriously consider either brown bag lunches (each person brings their own food) or potlucks (everyone brings food to share with everyone else).

One of the neat things about potlucks is that they are a miniature version of the ecosystem itself. Potlucks, like ecosystems, are about co-creation and collaboration.

It's an opportunity to make something and share it. And whether we're talking about food or knowledge, creating something and then telling a story about it are what an ecosystem is all about.

There's also just something about breaking bread together which helps people get to know one-another on an authentic, personal level. And when you can create that kind of intimacy in a community, the stronger it will become... and the faster you will be able to grow it.

Email Newsletters

With all of these events going on in your ecosystem, it can be hard for entrepreneurs to keep-up with what's happening.

While many people promote and manage their events on Facebook, it's still a good idea to utilize an email newsletter as well.

While you could easily create your own email list on Constant Contact or Mail Chimp, a great email newsletter tailored to ecosystems is StartupDigest. Visit StartupDigest.com to learn more.

Environments

Informal Spaces

Coffee Shops - You don't need an expensive, polished space to bring entrepreneurs together. In fact, places like coffee shops are fertile breeding grounds for entrepreneurship.

Restaurants – A technology group in our community began having meetings at a local deli. The deli enjoyed having them there, because they always bought dinner.

Libraries – Many times libraries have private meeting rooms available for use. Some libraries have now began providing code camps for kids.

Existing companies – An existing company may have an innovation lab, or allow startup groups to hold meetings in their conference rooms. If there's a particularly innovative company in your community, reach-out to see if you can learn more about their facility.

Formal Spaces (Incubators, Accelerators, and Coworking)

While entrepreneurs can make all kinds of connections at events and online, an ecosystem still benefits from their close physical proximity to one-another on a consistent basis. For this reason, you need to make sure your community includes a place for entrepreneurs to be around one another.

Now, I'll admit that I'm a little bias on this

topic. I've been an incubator manager for a long time. And during that time I've heard opinions from others on their perceived effectiveness and ineffectiveness of these kind of facilities.

But I can tell you from first-hand experience that when these facilities are run well they can make an immeasurable impact on the success of the entrepreneurs who are in the building.

Let's take a look at the primary differences between incubators, accelerators, and coworking spaces. While virtual versions also exist for each of these, we are talking here about examples with physical buildings and structures.

Incubators - A business incubator is a facility where entrepreneurs rent space to launch their company, while also receiving support services such as group training, individual mentoring, shared equipment, networking opportunities, and connections to financial capital.

Companies are only located within the

facility for a limited period of time (sometimes ranging from 1-3 years). Incubators exist to serve a wide variety of industries, including technology, manufacturing, healthcare, retail, fashion, culinary, and more. More information at www.iNBIA.org

Accelerators - A business accelerator usually has a much shorter interaction initially with companies than that of an incubator. Many accelerator programs, like TechStars for example, develop early stage companies over the span of a few months in "cohorts" rather than years.

These are almost always tech startups, since they are able to scale in that short of a timeframe. Rather than charge a rent or program fee like incubators, it's not uncommon for accelerators to take equity in the companies they are working with. More information at www.gan.co

Coworking Spaces - If you've ever met an entrepreneur or a freelancer who was able to work from home or a coffee shop, and all they really needed was a Wi-Fi connection, desk space for the day, coffee, and other people to interact with occasionally, that's what coworking is about.

While coworking spaces don't typically have an education or programming aspect like incubators or accelerators, they are an affordable option for the entrepreneur or small startup who wants to get out of their home and work in a more professional setting.

While some smaller coworking centers are independent, coworking companies exist like WeWork which are often found in larger cities. More information at both www.WeWork.com and www.GlobalWorkspace.org

Other types of physical places for entrepreneurs include ones that are more specific to a particular industry or niche. Examples: culinary or commissary kitchens for food entrepreneurs and makerspaces for inventors of physical products.

One of the recent trends we've seen in ecosystems over the last few years is a combining of two or more of these types of spaces into one. For instance, many incubator programs include either an accelerator program or coworking space as well.

Go Global

One of the best ways to "hack" your ecosystem and make it grow faster is by connecting the entrepreneurs in it to the global marketplace. If you have startups that aren't focusing on global markets to find customers, investors, partners, etc., help them go after those connections!

Checkout Global Entrepreneurship Week for ideas on how to get your ecosystem on the global stage www.genglobal.org

A Final Word on Synergy

Entrepreneurs often suffer from loneliness. So, do the ecosystem builders who serve them.

When we put entrepreneurs and ecosystem builders in physical proximity to one-another regularly, we create not only opportunities for mutual understanding and friendship, but also for collaborative innovation.

And that's the glue that holds entrepreneur

ecosystems together and makes them grow.

5 Action Checklist

☐ Set a goal of making **10 introductions each day.** Track these introductions in a journal or spreadsheet. Follow-up on introductions, see if the connection was actually made, and if any value resulted. Track that value as a benchmark for yourself and for potential testimonials down the road.

☐ Apply to become a 1 Million Cups community (free) or at the least **create a weekly event** so that entrepreneurs have an opportunity for regular contact in a large-group setting and support one-another.

☐ **Create a regular competition or pitch event.** "Gamify" entrepreneurship. People enjoy competing with one-another and watching others compete. These events not only make entrepreneurship fun, but they help form connections!

☐ **Decide what kind of space(s) will be dedicated to entrepreneurs.** Is an informal space (coffee shop) or a formal space (incubator, accelerator, or co-working center) right for your community? How will all of the pieces fit together?

If you need help making this determination, please reach-out to me at Ryan@RyanLilly.com

If I'm not able to help, I have a network of friends who specialize in determining what kinds of programs might work best in your unique ecosystem.

☐ **Make connections outside your ecosystem**, so that you can help entrepreneurs achieve a global reach. Sign-up to participate in Global Entrepreneurship Week (GEW), contact your state's trade office, or see if there is a need for ecommerce training in your community so that businesses can sell more online.

5 SUPPORT

Support - Start by listening!

How many world-changing ideas have never gone anywhere because either someone wasn't brave enough to share, or someone wasn't empathetic enough to listen?

Remember what it feels like to have a great idea and to want to share that with someone. Now, consider how valuable it would be to become someone who truly listens to new ideas.

Entrepreneurs must be heard before they

can be helped; connected before they can be catapulted to success.

After seeking-out and synergizing entrepreneurs together, as ecosystem builders we have to find the most effective ways to support them.

With each entrepreneur you meet, **LISTEN** to them and **THEN** ask yourself:

"What or whom do they need most right now, and how can I connect them to that thing or that person?"

Then do it on the spot.

On a larger scale, there isn't a one-size-fits-all answer on how to do this.

And you have to start by listening to what entrepreneurs in your community are consistently asking for.

Start to notice patterns of needs. Then go out and systematically solve them.

Remember, a community's ability to

succeed in this new economy will be directly determined by its ability to connect and serve people who take action on new ideas -- their ability to actually support the entrepreneurs that call their community home.

Small Businesses vs. Startups

There's an important difference between small businesses and startups.

The people behind both small businesses and startups are entrepreneurs, but there is a big distinction to be made here which will allow you to support and serve each of them better.

You might think of **small businesses** as the mom-and-pops in your community. They're often slow-to-incremental in growth and sometimes they're considered "lifestyle" businesses.

Small businesses sell existing products or services in traditional industries. You can think of a small business as, in a way, a hearty freshwater fish.

Now small business is very risky. There's the statistic that 50% of small businesses fail after five years in business. But relatively speaking, compared to startups, they're more hardy fish.

They're often financed by the owner or maybe a loan from a bank. They're prevalent in both rural and urban environments.

A **startup** on the other hand is one with an innovative product or service which may also be in an emerging, unproven industry or marketplace.

There's a great definition provided by Steve Blank who says a startup is, "… a temporary organization used to search for a repeatable and scalable business model."

Staying with our analogy, startups are more like delicate tropical fish. Startups may receive equity capital.

They sometimes work with angel investors and in very rare cases venture capitalists.

Startups are often rarer in rural environments.

One of these "fish" is not better than the other. The goal is to have both in your ecosystem and to have that diversity.

Think about what it takes to support each of these types of fish. To support small businesses (a freshwater fish), you need a clean tank and some food.

Startups (tropical fish) on the other hand, require a lot more care.

Once, I wanted to have a tropical fish tank in our home. I had never had tropical fish before but my wife had them growing up.

She said, "You know, you really have to

have a lot of stuff to take care of those guys. It's not just as simple as giving him some food and making sure their water is clean.

There's all this extra stuff you must have to make sure that the environment is right for them. You must monitor the temperature, the pH, and the salinity.

You have to have a good filter, you have to have coral in there for them, and they need special food!"

That might be a good analogy for you as you think about really supporting high growth startups. The environment, or the ecosystem, is the key. And there are more environmental factors that need to be just right.

Recently, we went to a large aquarium together. A tour guide said the following about the tropical fish, which really hit-home for me as an entrepreneurial ecosystem builder…

"The health of these fish is a direct reflection of the health of their environment. If the coral is healthy, so are the fish. If the fish are not healthy, neither is the coral."

The success of the entrepreneurs in your ecosystem is in part a reflection of the quality of their environment. And sometimes you're going to need to help scrub the slime off the glass.

Leaders and Feeders

I referred earlier to Brad Feld's book, *Startup Communities*. One of the most important distinctions he makes is that of leaders vs. feeders in an entrepreneurial ecosystem.

The leaders must be the entrepreneurs.

The feeders are those who feed entrepreneurs the nutrients they need. Schools, government, and other institutions exist to serve entrepreneurs, not to lead them.

When institutions like universities and government try to <u>lead</u> entrepreneurship development efforts, rather than to <u>support or feed</u> those efforts, things usually don't go well.

Remember, keep entrepreneurs in the driver's seat!

Listening

Sometimes just listening to entrepreneurs helps them work through their own problems. I can't tell you how many times I've been sitting with an entrepreneur and they'll start telling me about what problem(s) they're facing..

And then, all of the sudden, they have an "Aha" moment on their own.

"Hmm, you know what? That's probably what I should do about that!" they'll say.

I believe that many times entrepreneurs already know all of the answers deep-down. Sometimes fear or chaos get in the way for them of seeing that answer.

Sometimes, they just need someone like you to listen to them.

Questions

Questions are powerful. When meeting with an entrepreneur, you shouldn't so much be giving them advice as you are asking them questions about what they're telling you.

Questions will not only help to clarify their business model for you, but it's also good practice for the entrepreneur to begin anticipating the questions they might be asked by customers or investors.

Questions also help you understand what level of development an entrepreneur is currently at, what they need right now, and may help elicit new ideas or opportunities the entrepreneur had not considered yet.

Most importantly (and sorry if this sounds cheesy), questions show you care. I once sat-in on a mentoring session where the entrepreneur told the mentor everything that was going on – then the mentor formed an assessment and spewed their thoughts all over them.

Make sure you're asking important questions throughout the conversation.

10 Sample Questions to Ask Entrepreneurs When You First Meet Them

There are a few questions that I ask every entrepreneur when I meet with them. I hope that the list of questions below provides you with some conversation starters the next time you meet with an entrepreneur.

1. What are you doing now for work, and how has this career led you into starting this business? Do you have any experience in what you're trying to do? Have you ever started in business before?

For example, if I meet an entrepreneur who tells me that she is going to start a coffee shop, yet she has no experience in ever having made coffee or worked in a shop, I might suggest that she spend some time in one first.

2. What is your "why" for starting this business? What passion do you have for this product or service?

3. What is the outcome you are hoping to achieve? Are you building a company with hopes of an acquisition within a few years, or is this a lifestyle business that you plan on having until you one day retire?

4. Tell me about your idea. What really makes this idea unique? How are you differentiating yourself from the competition? Besides saying that you will provide quality customer service and a low price, why should anyone care about what you have to offer? In other words, what's your core value proposition?

5. Describe to me who your ideal customer is. How are you reaching that target audience?

6. What have you done already to test your assumptions or bring your product or service to market? What have you learned so far? (This question also helps determine the entrepreneur's coachability and willingness to accept new information and pivot.)

7. What financial resources do you have available to you? How do you plan to start small and bootstrap this business verses taking on outside debt or equity to start?

8.   Who have you partnered with or will soon partner with to make this business successful? Who do you need to meet? Do you have a mentor and basic service providers like an accountant, a lawyer, and graphic designer?

9.   Are you clear on the next 3-5 steps you need to take towards starting and growing this business?

10. What challenges do you feel that you are facing, what fears do you have, and how can I help you overcome any of those? How can we help you?

Be sure that as you were asking these questions, they do not sound routine or monotonous. Display a genuine interest and excitement and the entrepreneur's ideas and help them achieve their desired outcomes.

Mentors

It's important to find mentors who have the right motivation when it comes to helping entrepreneurs.

Is the mentor in it for themselves - for the potential paid consulting clients, as an example?

Be sure to find people who genuinely care about growing your entrepreneurial community and helping the people who need it most. When you're interviewing mentors, ask them their "why" for doing this too.

Unfortunately, some mentors will have conflicts of interest with the entrepreneurs that they are paired with. It's important that you always get these out on the table and disclosed from the beginning.

For these reasons and more, if you create a formal mentoring program, it is important to have an agreement signed by mentors covering a general code of conduct and managing expectations on all sides.

Service Providers

It's important that entrepreneurs have connections to all of the necessary subject matter experts and service providers.

Be sure to build a network of the following professionals. They'll not only be important for introducing to entrepreneurs, but as discussed in Chapter 3, they will also send new entrepreneurs to you.

- Accountants
- Bankers & Investors
- Attorneys (Business Law & IP)
- Insurance
- Realtors
- Graphic Design/Marketing
- Programming/Development
- Prototyping
- Industry-Specific Consultants

Educate

Any workshop that you develop for entrepreneurs should be both needs-based and targeted.

It needs to be needs-based in that the workshop should be created only in response to a specific need that is being expressed by entrepreneurs in your community.

If entrepreneurs are repeatedly telling you that they're having an issue with some aspect of starting a business, that's a sign that some kind of workshop or program may need to be created around addressing that concern.

Unfortunately, some ecosystem builders make the mistake of creating programs simply because they have seen them in other communities or because they just "think" that it is something which demand exists for. This goes back to thinking like an entrepreneur in order to serve entrepreneurs.

We must first make sure that we are creating a product (in our case a workshop or a training) in response to a real need that exists for our customer (in our case, the customer is the entrepreneur).

When we say that a workshop or training is targeted, it means that we are thinking also about what kind of entrepreneur we are serving.

There are many kinds of entrepreneurs in an ecosystem, and not every training or workshop will be appropriate given their stage of growth, industry, etc. Therefore, the workshops and trainings we do create, should be targeted specifically at the people who are meant to use them.

If you created a workshop for culinary entrepreneurs, as an example, you would not want to market it through the same channels that you would trainings for tech entrepreneurs.

This is a common mistake that I see ecosystem builders making -- they are not using targeting in the right way to reach the entrepreneurs they are trying to serve.

Also make sure that these trainings are taught by actual, active entrepreneurs with personal, relevant experience whenever possible.

Rather than to create a new training program from scratch, here are two excellent entrepreneur training courses to consider customizing to your community:

Kauffman FastTrac – Developed over the last 25 years, FastTrac "equips aspiring entrepreneurs with the business skills and insights, tools, resources, and peer networks necessary to start and grow successful businesses."

Entrepreneurs can take the course self-paced online for free – or you can opt to become a FastTrac Affiliate community and facilitate the courses in-person or online in your town or city.

(As a side note, I recently became a FastTrac Program Manager and a trained Facilitator. The content is awesome!)

More info at www.fasttrac.org

Costarters.Co – This program "equips grassroots leaders with the best tools and resources needed to support starters of all kinds, fueling vibrant entrepreneurial ecosystems."

While I've never experienced the Co.Starters program for myself, I have met other ecosystem builders who speak very highly of it.

More info at https://costarters.co/

Engage

Whenever possible, you want to co-create the support structure you're putting together with your ecosystem building team.

These education programs should never be dependent on one person or even a handful of people. The ecosystem itself should be engaged in providing these trainings.

An ecosystem builder can support an education effort in the short-term, but long-term sustainability of a program is determined by how engaged the broader community has become, whether the education process is systematized, and whether there is buy-in and ownership of the program from entrepreneurs in the ecosystem itself.

In other words, don't let it be you standing-up to teach a class! Your job is to find the experts.

Empower

So many entrepreneurs just need someone

to listen to them and encourage their progress.

Here are 5 important considerations when meeting with an entrepreneur for the first time.

1.   The entrepreneur is coming to you and **trusting you** with their idea. They might have never started a business before, and at some level they're fearful.

Telling someone about an idea that you have puts you in a vulnerable place. An entrepreneur may have many concerns about telling you their idea, including that you might share it, steal it yourself, or ridicule it.

It can be helpful at the outset of your conversation to clear the air.

Let the entrepreneur know that your confidential conversation won't go beyond the walls of your meeting space, and that you promise to give them open and professional feedback no matter how crazy the concept.

I'm not a fan of signing non-disclosure agreements (NDAs). As an IP attorney once told me, "NDA's are written to be litigated." Instead, create a relationship of trust and a reputation for keeping your word. And you don't always need to know the inter-workings of their secret sauce to help them.

2. **Listen more than you talk.**

See the previous chapter for more on this. It's important, so it's worth mentioning again!

3. What's the **"adjacent possible"** for this entrepreneur's idea? What else could they do with this idea, that they may not be thinking of? Who else could they partner with in my ecosystem?

4. Sometimes, it's not a bad idea to do some **due diligence** on the entrepreneur before you meet with them. Google them. Is there anything online about them that would be helpful or add context for you during the conversation?

If you're going to be introducing this person to others, are you confident in their reputation, credibility, and work ethic?

5. Give them encouragement! Even if you dislike the idea, encourage them towards testing it. Even if they've just tested an idea and failed, encourage them towards trying again. **Be an encourager.** You might be the only one they have.

On that note of encouragement, if you're someone passionate about empowering entrepreneurs, be sure to checkout the Startup Champions Network. www.StartupChampions.co

Put yourself in the entrepreneur's shoes and at all times be empathetic towards what they're trying to accomplish.

5 Action Checklist

☐ With your team, **identify 3 patterns of questions** that entrepreneurs keep asking in your community. Then, identify ways that education or other support could help address them once and for all.

☐ Who are the most influential entrepreneurial leaders and institutional feeders in your community? **List 5 of each.** Discuss how you can better incorporate them into your ecosystem.

☐ If you don't yet have a mentor network, **brainstorm a list of 10 successful entrepreneurs who could serve as mentors**. If you already have a mentor network, brainstorm 10 new potential reach-outs.

☐ In a Google Doc or other easily-sharable document, **make a list of service providers** (examples: attorneys and accountants) which your organizing team has had positive, direct experience with. Make sure this can be easily shared with entrepreneurs when they need it.

☐ Become a Kauffman FastTrac or Co.Starters Affiliate. **<u>Begin teaching some kind of entrepreneurship education course in your ecosystem.</u>**

6 STREAMLINE

I was boarding a bus for a tour of the Kansas City entrepreneur ecosystem. The tour was hosted by the Kansas City Startup Foundation, and it would turn-out to be one of the most impressive community tours I've ever been on.

After coming-out of the hotel and lining-up to board the buses, I noticed a gentleman next to me whose name badge indicated he worked in Kansas City government. Having worked in city government in the past myself, I thought it would be interesting to ask him a few questions.

"From a city government perspective, what would you most attribute the growth of your small business and startup communities to?" I said.

The city official didn't even have to think about his reply. He responded immediately with, "We got out of the way."

"Got out of the way?" I said. "What do you mean?"

"We made starting a business here as easy as it could be. We found out what challenges entrepreneurs were having, in regards to dealing with the city, and we worked to either eliminate those things or make them really easy to understand."

The city official's answer struck me as both simple and profound. As I boarded the bus I wondered to myself, "How many cities are out there thinking they have to create this elaborate system and all of these programs to serve entrepreneurs, when in reality one of the best things they can do is just find ways to 'get out of the way?"

I could immediately see how many communities would resist such an idea. Sometimes, in an effort to help entrepreneurs, they just end-up creating more bureaucracy, more red-tape for them to go-through.

They might have good intentions, don't get me wrong. But those intentions create unintended consequences for entrepreneurs who just need to get from point A to point B as quickly as possible.

Regarding the benefits of "getting out of the way," I've since found the same to be true for educational and non-profit institutions as well.

Many times universities and local non-profits will create entrepreneurship programs which end-up doing more harm than good for entrepreneurs.

So, for these reasons, after you've sought-out entrepreneurs, brought them together, and found ways to support them based on their needs, you have to next fill one of the biggest needs of all -- to streamline their environment.

Take-away what entrepreneurs don't need, and make those things left over as easy as possible for them to maneuver around.

Creating systems to support entrepreneurs involves bulldozing barriers, and entrepreneurs don't always have the time or influence to drive the bulldozers.

If you can do this, I can guarantee your community won't get left-behind at the bus stop.

Eliminate (Destroy what doesn't work)

Prioritize: Some things will be faster to eliminate than others. Where do the most urgent pain points exist for entrepreneurs in your ecosystem?

Who will you need to help eliminate this? Are politics involved?

Businesses once operated in structural hierarchies and strict procedure. Today, that hierarchy is flattened and a company is free-flowing and organic.

Our institutions, including government and education, must adapt as well in order to serve entrepreneurs. Right now, those old-school bureaucratic practices are some of the biggest stumbling blocks for entrepreneurs.

And maybe some of those pain points and bureaucratic hurdles don't involve government at all. Maybe they have to do with navigating some other process or another type of institution. Whatever it is, find a way of eliminating it and you'll be making your ecosystem that much stronger.

And when it comes to destroying those barriers, know that you'll probably make a few people angry.

But know that as an ecosystem builder, if you're not making at least one person angry, you're probably not creating meaningful-enough change.

Engineer (Create easy SYSTEMS)

Think innovatively to create systems which make entrepreneur's lives easier. How could you leverage technology to solve a problem they face? Maybe it's not even a technological system you need to create, but a manual one which can increase your ecosystem's efficiency?

Escort (Take them by the hand)

The personal touch! Much of helping entrepreneurs involves individual hand holding. Whether it's personal introductions to other entrepreneurs in your community, or helping an entrepreneur overcome some barrier, there are some things which simply cannot be systematized and require a personal and caring approach.

There is, however, a balance here in that you should never do for an entrepreneur what day should or could do for themselves. Be sure that you are "teaching them how to fish" verses fishing for them. In the former scenario you'll be setting them up for success, in the ladder you will be doing nothing but an injustice.

One great idea/resource we adopted in my community was that of a "Hitchhiker's Guide" document. Modeled after the "Hitchhiker's Guide to the Kansas City Startup Ecosystem" this online document is a one-stop guidebook for anyone launching a business in our community.

You can see the one we created at www.OcalaStartupGuide.com

It's really pretty simple – the Hitchhiker's Guide is a Google Slide deck which we constantly update with resources for local entrepreneurs. It can be viewed by anyone at any time, and the slide format makes it easy to navigate through.

This guide is the perfect example of something that has saved us so much time an energy. We used to get constant requests for some of the information contained in it (for example, a listing of local patent attorneys.)

Each time I would have to go and look the information up, and then put it in an email.

Now I just send them to the website link which leads to the always-up-to-date slide deck! I recommend every community have something like this – especially in-place of printed resource books which almost immediately become outdated the day they are printed.

A final word on eliminating barriers / streamlining:

An entrepreneurial community is held-together by a fabric of intricate connections. A community stuck in the past is torn-apart by its own barriers and bureaucracies.

Indeed, a community can be its own worst enemy economically.

5 Action Checklist

☐ What 3 things most need to be **eliminated**?

☐ What 3 things most need to be **engineered**? (Created to minimize bureaucracy).

☐ What 3 things do entrepreneurs most need to be better **escorted through**?

☐ Create a **Hitchhiker's Guide** or similar document (see example).

☐ **What barriers do you see potentially popping-up in the future** for your ecosystem? How can you begin addressing them now?

7 SHARE

At conferences like the E-SHIP Summit, where I meet other ecosystem builders, I'm always amazed at how humble people are about what they do to help entrepreneurs.

It's not uncommon that I'll meet someone, and they'll either not mention or somehow down-play the awesome things going-on in their ecosystem.

I once met a lady at one of these conferences we'll call Sarah. I had heard from several other people that Sarah had an outstanding program for young female

entrepreneurs.

Interested to learn more, I asked her about it. "Well, yeah, that thing," she started, "we're still trying to get it off the ground, there's a ton of problems with it, and we only have a couple of small success stories so far," she said. "It's really not much."

I get it. It doesn't feel polite to brag. But at the same time, one of the most important roles of an ecosystem builder is to tell stories.

The stories of successful companies.

The stories of failed companies who got back up and tried again.

The story of your community's ecosystem as a whole.

The story of where you've been, where you are, and where you're going as a community.

Recall from one of the first chapters in this book that as ecosystem builders we must be entrepreneurs ourselves, with entrepreneur mindsets, which includes at the core: selling!

We survive by selling, just like the entrepreneurs we're trying to help. And I'm convinced that the single most powerful way to sell is to tell stories.

So many of our entrepreneur ecosystems are like Sarah's. We have amazing things going-on in them, but the word isn't getting out.

If you're failing to get the word-out about entrepreneurship in your community, you're likely missing-out on the other would-be entrepreneurs in your ecosystem who would be inspired to start their own business if they only heard that story.

You're depriving the existing startups, who may be considering throwing-in-the-towel, of an inspirational story that may just make them decide to keep going.

Stories are the lifeblood of an entrepreneurial ecosystem. The better you can become at capturing and telling great stories, the more successful entrepreneurs in your community, and your ecosystem as a whole, will become.

So, if you're like Sarah, now is the time to get the message out any way you can, through every medium and channel available to you.

Tell the story. Because at the end of the day, stories are the greatest fuel available to you for accelerating the growth of your ecosystem.

Ideas for Capturing & Telling Stories

1. Video – YouTube & Facebook Live – Recordings of events in your ecosystem, success stories, etc.

2. One of the most underutilized marketing tactics in Ecosystem Building, or any field, is the testimonial. What companies are succeeding in your community, and how can you capture those stories and begin promoting them through all of your online channels?

3. Create a Podcast or news blog about your ecosystem. I once met a great example of a startup news site in the Midwest: www.SiliconPrairieNews.com

Some ecosystem builders do an awesome job at seeking-out, synergizing, supporting, and streamlining entrepreneurship, but they fail to share stories -- stories of both the entrepreneurs they've helped and their ecosystem's story as a whole.

Telling a great story about your ecosystem is important because it:

- Brings more exposure (and hopefully customers) to the entrepreneurs within the ecosystem
- Encourages other potential entrepreneurs in the community that they can do the same,
- Creates even greater opportunities for connections and resources for the ecosystem building team.

In other words, tell a single entrepreneur's story and you'll help them sell more stuff. Tell the collective story of a community of entrepreneurs and not only will they sell more stuff, but they'll sell entrepreneurship to new entrepreneurs in your community.

And maybe it's time your community change its story…

The path to economic vitality starts with evolving the mentality around existing reality. Sharing success stories is how we do that. Ecosystem Hacking entails quickly shifting a community's mindset through changing the stories it tells itself. In the process, the community creates a new identity.

And these stories don't have to be all sunshine and rainbows.

Communities shouldn't talk only of their successes, but also of the failures that led to those successes. In doing so, it will earn a reputation of both authenticity and innovative audacity – entrepreneurial fearlessness.

I once met an ecosystem builder from a rural part of Mexico. He told me how taboo it is in his town to be considered a failure at business – and how failure in a close-knit community like his often-meant shame and social alienation.

To combat this, he created a weekly meeting

called F-up Fridays (although I'm abbreviating here). The purpose of F-up Friday is to encourage entrepreneurs to talk openly about how they had failed that week – to not only make failure socially acceptable, but to congratulate those who had failed for even trying in the first place.

Elevate (Recognize Entrepreneurial Success)

Raise entrepreneurs up and make them feel like the heroes they are to your community.

Before something can be shared, it must first be shareable. Help entrepreneurs codify their message so that it spreads more easily. How can you also package stories together?

A few ideas on how to elevate entrepreneurs…

Awards programs are a great way to elevate success. See the section on this in Chapter 4.

Create **custom print-on-demand books** to tell the stories of your local entrepreneurs. Checkout www.InnovationHubUSA.com and https://amzn.to/2WpnZLj for examples.

Some communities get really creative with ways to recognize entrepreneurial success. Checkout what they did in Reno with creating a set of **playing cards** which feature local entrepreneurs: www.RenoStartupDeck.com

Espouse (Entrepreneurial beliefs - tell people who you are)

An entrepreneurial ecosystem not only has to define itself around a set of beliefs about entrepreneurship, but also espouse those beliefs on a regular basis.

In practical terms, this means creating a codifying a common mission in your community, living it, and retelling it every day in new ways -- both within the ecosystem (in order to keep entrepreneurs within the existing network engaged) and outside of it (in order to engage new entrepreneurs and grow the network).

In many respects, a startup ecosystem is a lot like a church. It's a place where people come to be reminded of and celebrate a common set of beliefs -- and also welcome new people into the fold. See the core values of the Kansas City Startup Village located at: www.KCStartupVillage.org

Embody (As a community - collectively become more of who you say you are)

The more that an ecosystem resembles its own mission and vision, the more authentic to itself it can be, the more magnetic it will be to entrepreneurs looking for a place they also can be themselves in.

Innovation and Storytelling are Connected

The more entrepreneurs there are in a local economy, the more that economy will innovate. The more it can innovate, tell a story, and attract other entrepreneurs, the longer it will survive.

5 Action Checklist

☐ **What's your ecosystem's unique story?** Similar to an elevator pitch, could you convey that story in a minute or less? Write it down.

☐ What are **three stories of successful entrepreneurs** in your area? How well do you know those 3 stories. Write them down. Collect stories like these in a journal or a Google Doc to share with others.

☐ Conduct a **Facebook Live interview**

☐ **Get one testimonial**, either written or on video, from an entrepreneur you've helped to connect to someone. Incorporate that testimonial somewhere into your marketing.

☐ **Get creative!** Look into creating a print-on-demand booklet of stories of local entrepreneurs, or something cool like the deck of playing cards mentioned above.

8 DIVERSITY

Last year I organized a lunch-and-learn event for Hispanic business owners in my community. We partnered with an organization that serves Hispanic businesses, and we provided our largest conference room free of charge to them.

Although the entire workshop was conducted in Spanish, and I don't speak Spanish myself, I actually stayed for the entire thing.

Honestly, I was mostly there for the free burritos, which we had purchased for the attendees from the best Mexican restaurant in town.

At the conclusion of the lunch, there was networking time for the attendees to get to know one-another. Again, I felt out-of-place not knowing Spanish, but I stuck-around the room to help clean-up and offer any help that I could.

A young entrepreneur named Roberto came-up to me.

In broken English he said, "This has meant a lot. This is the first time I've been able to connect with other entrepreneurs."

"Really?" I said. "You've never belonged to any local networking groups, the Chamber of Commerce, or anything like that?"

"No," Roberto said with a depressed look on his face. "I've never saw myself fitting-into those groups. There's no one else at those events who looks like me."

That last sentence has stuck with me since. "No one else at those events who looks like me."

So many times we take for granted how difficult it can be for minority groups to access various parts of our community and ecosystem.

At the core of it, we not only need to invite everyone (diversity) but also make them feel welcome and an active part of the conversation (inclusion).

My conversation with Roberto made me realize how many other people there must be in my community who don't come to our events because they don't see reflections of themselves in them.

When it comes to how to increase diversity within your ecosystem, there's no magic answer. But that day Roberto and I sat-down together to finish-off a second burrito. And sometimes sharing a meal together is the best place to start.

Two stats from the Kauffman Foundation E-SHIP Playbook that astound me every time I read them:

- Women are about half as likely to own businesses as men.
- Minorities own less than 20% of employer businesses and only 17.4% of businesses with revenue of at least $1 million.

While I certainly don't have a single, definitive answer on how to improve ecosystem diversity, here are five ideas to get started with:

1. **Start with Diverse Organizers** – One of the best things we did when building our 1 Million Cups organizer team was to make it intentionally diverse.

   In doing so, our audience each week reflected that diversity, because each of the organizers spread the word to their individual communities.

2. **Break Bread Together** – As mentioned earlier, food is a convener and builds friendship and trust. Create potlucks open to everyone, intentionally reach-out to people who may not typically get an invite, and make them feel genuinely

included in the conversation when they get there.

3. **Create Diversity Talks** – I heard this idea at a conference last year. One of the challenges to overcoming barriers related to diversity is that few like to talk about those barriers openly.

   You have to get diversity out into the open in order to really address it.

   For this reason, consider doing a series of Diversity Talks (podcasts or videos) with a diverse array of entrepreneurs in your community. What are the real-world challenges they face? It begins with getting it out in the open, no matter how uncomfortable that may be.

4. **Reach-out to Faith Communities** – Churches are a convening point and a community all their own. Speak to clergy in your community about what you're trying to do and see if they can help spread the word to their congregations.

5. **Remember:** The diversity and the health

of an ecosystem go hand-in-hand. I've never seen a coral reef made-up of only starfish. And if a starfish-only coral reef does exist, I bet it's boring as hell.

Diversity makes ecosystems come-alive!

5 Action Checklist

☐ **Commit** as an ecosystem team to make diversity an intentional priority.

☐ **Break bread.** Make them feel welcome an include them in the conversation.

☐ Get diversity challenges and stories **out in the open.**

☐ **Get into the shoes and world of someone unlike you** – talk to clergy in the faith communities around you.

☐ **"Bring the love"** to everyone you meet, regardless of who they are.

9 THIS WORK MATTERS

Save yourself the expensive SWOT analysis. Your community's strength is its innovators, its weakness; a collective resistance to change, its opportunity; reinvention, and its greatest threat; egos and bureaucracy standing in the way.

Remember:

Seek
Synergize
Support
Streamline
Share

Find entrepreneurs, connect them, help them, remove barriers, and tell their stories.

Do all of these things every day -- with the same passion the entrepreneurs you're helping have -- and your community will come to life with a passion all its own.

If you want your community to really thrive in this new economy, you must get intentional about helping entrepreneurs. The best time to do this was yesterday, and the second-best time is right now.

The road ahead of any Ecosystem Builder is not an easy one.

As an Ecosystem Hacker, trying to make all of this happen faster, you're sure to face unique challenges as well.

But don't give-up the fight.

Because this work matters.

Your community depends on it.

And it depends on you.

NOW WHAT?

Enroll in my Ecosystem Hacking course!

More information at www.RyanLilly.com

Invite me to speak at your next event or work one-on-one with your economic development or ecosystem team to achieve faster results!

Email me at Ryan@RyanLilly.com

www.ingramcontent.com/pod-product-compliance
Lightning Source LLC
Chambersburg PA
CBHW070931210326
41520CB00021B/6891